YOUR KNOWLEDGE HAS VALUE

Gebhard Deißler

Die Schwarzwälder Kirschtorte: Eine didaktische Metapher des Interkulturellen Managements

The Black Forest Cherry Cake: Metaphor Of Intercultural Management

GRIN Verlag

Bibliografische Information der Deutschen Nationalbibliothek:

Die Deutsche Bibliothek verzeichnet diese Publikation in der Deutschen National-
bibliografie; detaillierte bibliografische Daten sind im Internet über http://dnb.d-
nb.de/ abrufbar.

Imprint:

Copyright © 2013 GRIN Verlag GmbH
Druck und Bindung: Books on Demand GmbH, Norderstedt Germany
ISBN: 978-3-656-56624-3

This book at GRIN:

http://www.grin.com/en/e-book/229727/die-schwarzwaelder-kirschtorte-eine-
didaktische-metapher-des-interkulturellen

GRIN - Your knowledge has value

Der GRIN Verlag publiziert seit 1998 wissenschaftliche Arbeiten von Studenten, Hochschullehrern und anderen Akademikern als eBook und gedrucktes Buch. Die Verlagswebsite www.grin.com ist die ideale Plattform zur Veröffentlichung von Hausarbeiten, Abschlussarbeiten, wissenschaftlichen Aufsätzen, Dissertationen und Fachbüchern.

Visit us on the internet:

http://www.grin.com/

http://www.facebook.com/grincom

http://www.twitter.com/grin_com

Transcultural Management

Gebhard Deißler D.E.A./UNIV. PARIS I

DIE SCHWARZWÄLDER KIRSCHTORTE:

EINE DIDAKTISCHE METAPHER

DES INTERKULTURELLEN MANAGEMENTS

THE BLACK FOREST CHERRY CAKE METAPHOR OF INTERCULTURAL MANAGEMENT

CULTURE   RESEARCH

KULTUR FORSCHUNG

RECHERCHE CULTURE

BÚSQUEDA CULTURAL

RICERCA   CULTURALE

跨文化的智慧精髓

итранскультурная

Interkulturelles- u. Transkulturelles Management (German)

Intercultural &Transcultural Management (English)

Gestion Interculturelle et Gestion Transculturelle (French)

Gerencia Intercultural y Gerencia Transcultural (Spanish)

Gerência Intercultural e Gerência Transcultural (Portuguese)

跨文化的智慧精髓 - kua wen hua de zhi hui jing sui (Chinese)

транскультурная компетенция - transkulturnaja
kompetencija (Russian)

toransukaruchā　・manējimento (Japanese)
トランスカルチャー　・　マネジメント

Vishua Chaytana (Sanskrit)

ZAKAA AL-TA'ALOF AL-THAQAFEE (Arabic)

Index

I. The Black Forest Cherry Cake
Metaphor of Intercultural Management

Any cultural journey has a beginning and an end. An African proverb says that one always returns to one's own culture. The beginning and the end are circularly connected. On returning, however, one has a more differentiated perception of the place one has once left. Ideally one learns from the history of one's personal journey.
The time and cultures transcendent Christian Bible testifies to the immense learning provided by the personal traveling experience as well as to its risks and the need of an anchoring in God in the process. For only in Him all insoluble diversity related struggle and strive are resolved.

Reisen/Traveling

Sir 34,9	Wer viel gereist ist, hat reiches Wissen / und der Erfahrene redet verständig.
Sir 34,10	Wer nichts erfahren hat, weiß wenig, /
Sir 34,11	der Vielgereiste nimmt zu an Klugheit.
Sir 34,12	Vieles habe ich auf meinen Reisen gesehen, / viele Dinge habe ich durchgestanden.

Sir 34,13	Oft musste ich Todesgefahren bestehen, / aber ich wurde gerettet und sie gingen vorüber.
Sir 34,14	Der Geist der Gottesfürchtigen wird leben; /
Sir 34,15	denn ihr Hoffen ist auf ihren Retter gerichtet.
Sir 34,16	Wer den Herrn fürchtet, verzagt nicht / und hat keine Angst, denn der Herr ist seine Hoffnung.
Sir 34,17	Wohl dem, der den Herrn fürchtet. /
Sir 34,18	Auf wen vertraut er und wer ist seine Stütze?
Sir 34,19	Die Augen des Herrn ruhen auf denen, die ihn lieben; / er ist ein starker Schild, eine mächtige Stütze, / Schutz vor dem Glutwind, / Schatten in der Mittagshitze, / Halt vor dem Straucheln, Hilfe vor dem Fall,
Sir 34,20	Freude für das Herz, Licht für die Augen, / Heilung, Leben und Segen.

.

Hegel, whose birthplace is about 50 meters down the road from where I am writing these lines, maintains that „we learn from history that we learn nothing from it". Collectively that seems to hold and it seems to be due to our mental programming as we said previously. This idea has also been modeled by Heidegger in the „memory-anticipation" model, which is visualized in part II. One can logically explain it. Can one change it? The answer to this question is the tenor of my transcultural management approach, in which I identified a superordinate command and control function of the entire psycho-cultural architecture. See Transcultural Profiler or Management Model that integrates the generations of intercultural research and the Synopsis of Modern Intercultural Studies in part II. A solution to the problem articulated by the two great German philosophers! At the individual level one certainly can change if one is passionately enough committed to it. Change at the collective level requires what has been called a critical mass.

We can indeed evolve in circles, spiraling ever higher on our journeys. This has been said by the poet T. S. Eliot and quoted by one of the finest culture experts, namely Charles Hampden Turner in Building Cross-Cultural Competence:

> „We shall not cease from exploration
> And the end of all our exploring
> Will be to arrive where we started
> And know the place for the first time."

It is reflected in his dilemma theory. The double helix metaphor of synergy implies that at every turn of the helix a more sophisticated fine tuning of interfacing cultures occurs.

I have been using circle metaphors repeatedly in Transcultural Management – Transkulturelles Management, 2009, from where this chapter is taken: The 360° synergy model, visualized in part II, illustrates that we can achieve the highest synergy by leveraging the totality of the potentiality inherent in the full circle 360°. In other writing I have likened culture and the highest cultural wisdom to a circle. When the centre and periphery engage, the cultural diversity issues come to a term. One can cluster the world's cultures as a cake as has been done by the British management scholars Hickson and Pugh. And on closing the circle of the intellectual culture journey here and now it is befitting to draw once more on a circular metaphor which concretizes and grounds the lofty insight into what I have called the highest cultural wisdom. My here and now is the capital of the Land (federal state) of Baden-Württemberg. One of the well-known culinary specialties of the region of the Black Forest in Baden - which was politically united with Baden Württemberg half a century ago and whose diverse cultures lack full integration - is the Black Forest Cherry Cake (Schwarzwälder Kirschtorte). However, another internationally known cultural artifact of the same region is the Black Forest Clock. Both are very à propos in the sense that they are local cultural highlights and metaphors to practically concretize this approach to culture.

The Black Forest clock serves as a circular, cyclical metaphor of the culture journey and intercultural evolution and development. At a personal level this timeless artifact for the measurement of time symbolizes the closing of a circle in time and space, the reintegration into my home culture, which is the Land of Baden, its northern part. The Clock is typical of the southern part of Baden, where the Black Forest is located.

The famous local clock with the indigenous Black Forest cuckoo telling the hours, symbolizes the closing of the circle of the journey in time and space close to where it began long ago. Based on T. S. Eliot

> "I arrive where I started
> And know the place for the first time"

which means that I have a new awareness of an old place. The Black Forest Cherry Cake on the other hand combines, as a three dimensional circular culinary artifact, what has been said above about the circular conceptualization of culture, with a pragmatic understanding of the meaning of culture. This local coffee party patisserie specialty can teach us a lot about culture. It is a didactic instrument, simple, and everybody can relate to it, at least in this part of the world. It provides a local cultural and concrete approach to a universal, abstract phenomenon which constitutes a challenge to awareness. As such it can bridge the concrete and the abstract in a familiar way.

The main design features - inner and outer - of the gateau is that it constitutes a monoblock flat cylindrical whole, with a seamless coating of white cream and some 12 cherries circularly disposed to mark the slices for cutting and serving. The inner structure and composition highlights a system of layers, while the cherry forms the top of each multi-layer slice. The 12 ocataves transcultural management model, depicted in part II, can easily be represented by these vertical layers of cherry, whipping cream, chocolate, marmalade, dark sponge mixture etc. Thus, as in the twelve octaves transcultural management model we have an approximately 12 times 12 dimensional integrative model of the totality of culture and the management of cultures, based on the principle of functional integration and subordination. The touch of liquor, of spirit (cherry brandy) which permeates the entire cake and provides its unique flavour, can be likened to the noetic integrative spirit of the 3D model which is required to successfully manage transculturally. Thus we have added a culinary model of culture that is accessible to the child as well as to the manager. And as an exquisite patisserie which is truly delightful it can prepare a terrain suggestive not of the plight of transcultural managerial challenges but rather one of delight.

This localized approach to the intercultural world in its totality, the entire cake, is reconciliatory in its very essence and from the very start. Such a conceptualization and pedagogical tool can teach culture in an unthreatening way, as it conveys a sense of sociability in a homy atmosphere. The entire cultural edifice is naturally grafted onto the symbolical cultural roots and rituals embodied by the Black Forest Cherry Cake culture metaphor. People from other cultures may use their culture typical analog with similar engrafting and integrative effectiveness. As everyone has a different cultural background s/he will have to customize the culture edifice to his own cultural roots in order to maintain his or her cultural integrity while opening up to the process of intercultural evolution and transcultural management imperatives.

II. INTERCULTURAL MANAGEMENT INSTRUMENTS

(1) The ORJI Model (Ed Schein) – Observation-Emotional Response-Judgement-Initiative - highlights the importance of continuous checking and questioning routines in intercultural encounters in order to effectively manage intrapsychic processes.

(2) The MIS (misperception-misinterpretation-misevaluation) Factor Process (N. Adler) highlights the culture contingency of perception and how it is processed. Empathy and cybernetic thinking to manage the diverse perceptual cultural filters are helpful.

(3) The PIE (perception-interpretation-evaluation) Metaphor highlights the need that the various phases of the intrapsychic process management in the intercultural interfacing process must be kept apart.

The integration of items 1-3 is visualized in a multi-model on the following page.

The application of all instruments can be greatly enhanced if they are correlated to what has been shown in other chapters. They are to be contextualized in a superordinate understanding of culture with all-integrative impact, i.e. the inter-transcultural complementarity that underpins a metaphorical "quantum cultural effect".

Culture and Self: Multi-Modelling Intrapsychic Processes

ORJI-Cycle	Traps	Routines	Mis-Factor Effect	PIE-Metaphor
Observation	Misperception	Identify bases of misperception 1cultural assumptions 2personal defensive filters 3situational expectations	Misperception 1cultural filters distort	Perception
Emotional Reaction	Inappropriate emotional response	Identify own emotional response biases	Misinterpretation 1cross-cultural misca- tegorization 2stereotyping 3lack of cultural self- awareness 4projected similarity	Interpre-tation
Judgement	Rational analysis & judgement based on incorrect data	Identify cultural assumptions in judgement and reason	Cross-cultural Misevaluation 1judgements are strongly evaluative	Evaluation
Intervention	Intervening on seemingly correct judgement that is in fact incorrect	Systematic checking routines (questioning, listening, general spirit of inquiry)	Mistrust 1negative expectations	

Solutions/Measures	Checking Routines	Cybernetic thinking	Separating phases

Based on Nancy Adler, Ed Schein and Nigel Ewington

(4) The aggregate models of culture (ex. Hofstede) highlight the fact that there is a cultural pre-programming. This knowledge allows predicting and adapting to attitudes, values and behaviours if used flexibly and accounting for variances around a mean. It results in "culturally normals" (average expression of the cultural value preferences), "culturally hypernormals" (above average expression-) and "culturally marginal" (below average expression of cultural value preferences). It further results in the understanding of culture as a stereotype (assuming that all members of a culture express their cultural value preferences in a stereotypical way) or culture as a prototype (allowing for variation). See item 6.

(5) Dilemma theory (Adler and Trompenaars and Hampden-Turner) highlights the possibility of creating synergies from conflicting values based on the multi-step process for dilemma resolution of these authors. Details on this can be found in the authors' literature or in other texts by the writer of this text.

(6) The interpretivist paradigm or the negotiated culture approach (Brannen and Salk) highlights the assumption that aggregate models of culture as those of Hofstede and Trompenaars and Hampden Turner have limited predictive power as cultures are normal distributions, prototypes rather than stereotypes. This differentiation and additionally accounting for a maximum amount of contextual variables allows a dynamic approach to the management of emergent organizational cultures. - Items 4, 5 and 6 - the brief history of intercultural research - are summed up from a paradigmatic point of view in the last item of the present synopsis.

(7) Fusion: This strategy allows for the simultaneous existence of more than one cultural approach with the benefit that one may provide initially unsuspected

feedback and a complement to the other. - But Fusion can also be understood as a return to the source of life, where neither time nor space, nor thought nor person A nor person B, everything and nothing, exist. Here culture and its barriers do not arise. Cultural differences may at times be perceived as increasing interpersonal distance and thereby creating an additional obstacle to the deep-rooted need of fusion, of oneness with life itself. The awareness of the relevance of fusion may in some instances defuse culturally induced confusion... Though it may seem necessary at times to create distance, an ultimate Christian rationale also is Unity: "Ut unum sint", Christ Himself says to God the Father: "That all of them may be one, Father, just as you are in me and I am in you.. ." (John 17 : 21). Integral individuals mystically one?

(8) When in Rome do as the Romans do. This is a more general approach and adage which does not stick rigidly to the home culture, while the next approach number 9 places great store on the home culture while it borrows useful elements of target cultural environment.

(9) Cross-fertilization: Builds on the biological principle of adaptation for survival. In this sense a globalizing corporation may adopt some of the DNA of another culture to navigate challenging phases and environments.

(10)To the Greek become a Greek. This is the precept of Saint Paul, a Christian approach, which can be said to be the royal path to winning people's hearts and minds.

(11)In-depth understanding that literally sees through the game of culture in the sense that in certain cases each culture positions itself as the absolute and thereby relativizes the other culture and frequently expects her to pay the cost of the interfacing process.

(12)The art of seeing. Choiceless awareness (J. Krishnamurti). It complements cognitive seeing through a situation or someone by the art of pure perception with its own mental hygiene and power.

(13)Consciousness evolution and cultural development diagnostic (Dr. Th. Brosse and M. Bennett). See Evolution Profile in the Transcultural Management Profiler. The human evolution and the intercultural development stages allow a quick diagnostic as to the possible range of attitudes values and behaviours.

(14)Transcultural or noetic intelligence. This approach is based on the highest functions of a threefold hierarchical holistic architecture of man; from bottom to top: (1) the somatic, (2) the psychic and (3) the noetic. This three-level architecture of man features a top to bottom integration and control logic. Cultural conditioning is stored in the psychic level, the mind. Based on the neurophysiologic hierarchical integration and control principle, the noetic or transcultural level integrates the mental or cultural level.

(15)Culture is all about experiencing relationships - with oneself, others, the visible and the invisible environment -. Consider whether culture is used as a pretext to feed greed in relationships. How much culture does the (healthy) self and selflessness require? Culture can be strongly relativized by the self: from fundamentalism to quantité négligeable.

(16)Strive to establish your identity, physical as well as metaphysical, through true (self-) knowledge, which enfolds and transcends cultural conditioning, as taught by the   world's traditions and expressed in Greek as "Gnothi seauton", in Latin as "Nosce te ipsum", in Sanskrit as "Vidya", in the Christian tradition, the epistles of St. Paul contain informative metaphors about the nature of man and his relationship with his fellow man and the divine. Self-awareness training in western management education is a step in this direction.

(17)Ascertain the guiding cultural metaphor. Metaphors tend to subtly shape cultural patterns: Find out what metaphor best subsumes values, attitudes and behaviours in a culture. The sports metaphor, for example, with its emphasis on speed, individual competition and the quest for being number one seems to be the overriding motive that is replicated in the various social subsystems in America, the household and family metaphor is a forma mentis, which represents an attitudinal and behavioural leitmotif in parts of Asia, where Confucian ethics hold that the "family is the prototype of all social organization" and therefore emphasizes harmony, hierarchy and tradeoffs between seniors and juniors. The symphony orchestra metaphor seems to be a subtly governing motive of German culture which highlights a need for order and direction as displayed in a conductor who orchestrates a synergistic collective effort.

(18)Organisational behaviour metaphors: The above metaphors can be correlated to another set of empirically derived organisational behaviour metaphors, referred to as implicit organisational models by intercultural scholars, such as the village market for Anglo and Nordic cultures which emphasizes a pattern of individual achievement along with weak formalization. Germanic cultures highlight the culturally distinctive feature of formalized order, the Human Pyramid highlights the distinctive feature of authority residing in the leader and in formal rules as in Latin countries and last but not least, the Tribal or Family metaphor highlights the centralisation of power at the top.

(19)Cultivate a spirit of learning! Man is endowed with great freedom, which may challenge any predictions.

(20) Quantum-optical culture consciousness (neologism) which permits complementary vistas of culture and provides a more complete perception of cultural issues and therefore greater effectiveness in its management. (See quantum cultural approach to international diversity management by the author of this exposé)

(21) S. Ting-Toomey, G. Hofstede, E. Marx and R. Brislin and others provide valuable research on the entire expatriation-repatriation cycles from many angles to support intercultural transfers and transitions.

(22) M. Bennett's IDM or intercultural development model models and describes the phases and stages of intercultural sensitivity development; by three ethnocentric stages followed by three ethnorelative stages.

(23) CAGE Analysis by P. Ghemawat (Harvard Business Review) provides a differentiated model for distance analysis to support international decision making. This distance model distinguishes cultural (C), administrative, geographic and economic distance to provide a more precise notion of distance.

(Here follow a few concepts in German in order to apply complementary linguistic approaches to create a wider space of mind and consciousness conducive to enhanced intercultural perception.)

(24) Naturwissenschaftliche, als Metaphern verwendete Prinzipen aus den Bereichen der Quantenphysik, der Mikrobiologie, der Neurophysiologie u. der Kybernetik etc., die das Verständnis des Managements des Kulturellen erschließen. (Siehe den 5D/5P - Physik Metaphysik, Psychologie, Physiologie, Philosophie - erweiterten inter-transkulturellen Managementansatz):

1. Das Komplementaritätsprinzip Niels Bohrs
2. Die Heisenbergsche Unschärferelation
3. Die Doppelhelix der DNA
4. Das neurophysiologische Prinzip der funktionellen Subordination
5. Das neurophysiologische Prinzip der strukturellen Integration
6. Die psychosomatische Dualität
7. Die ganzheitliche dreifältige, noetisch-psycho-somatische Struktur des Menschen. Der Begriff „noetisch" bezeichnet hier die höchste Ebene der dreifältigen menschlichen Struktur.

8. Das Dao der Kultur

9. Die quantenkulturelle Axiomatik und der quantenkulturelle Effekt

10. Der transkulturelle Autopilot

11. Inter-transkulturelle Energetik: Potentialisierungs-
    Aktualisierungsdynamismus

12. Das Involutions-Evolutionsprinzip (auf einige dieser Prinzipien wird in
    anderen Texten Bezug genommen)

(25) Die transkulturelle Lingua Franca. Sie entsteht im Wege der Erkenntnis der
oberen Dimensionen des transkulturellen Profilers.

(26) Vidya (Sanskrit für Wissen), Gnothi seauton (Griechisch für Selbsterkenntnis),
Nosce te ipsum (Latein für Selbsterkenntnis), self-awareness (Englisch für
Selbstbewusstheit); während die Phasen Bewusstsein – Wissen – Kompetenzen den
klassischen Algorithmus des interkulturellen Kompetenzerwerbs bilden, geht der
transkulturelle Managementkompetenzerwerb von einer höheren Spiralwindung
interkultureller Selbstbewusstheit und Erkenntnis, einer höheren Form des
Bewusstseins und der Erkenntnis der Wahrheit als Bedingung für den
transkulturellen Kompetenzerwerb und der transkulturellen Intelligenz aus. Im
Fernen Osten sind das japanische Hishiryo Konzept, das chinesische Wuwei, sowie
das indische Konzept des Bewusstseins-Zeugen gleichermaßen kulturübergreifende
erkenntnistheoretische Wegweiser hin zu einer transkulturellen Dimension.

(27) „Por debajo de todo nuestro edificio está la libertad": Diese Formel der
spanischen Sartre-Schülerin Gloria Quevedo bedeutet: Unter unserem gesamten

Gebäude befindet sich die Freiheit. Im Bewusstsein dieser Erkenntnis gelangt man auch zur transkulturellen Intelligenz. Die Spitze und die Basis des transkulturellen Profiler Gebäudes gründen gleichermaßen in einem konditionierungsfreien Raum des Bewusstseins, der das gesamte kulturelle Gebäude trägt.

(28) Das Gebot der Liebe (caritas, agape) als Panaceum aller menschlichen Beziehungen.

(29) „Vor c'est faire" ein französisches Sprichwort, identisch mit Krishnamurtis Dictum "Seeing is doing", in der Bedeutung von Sehen ist Handeln kann mit Hilfe der Komplementaritätsprinzip Metapher als quantenkultureller Effekt (im übertragenen Sinn) übersetzt werden und zwar in dem Sinn, dass die Positionierung im Bewusstsein des Subjekts aktives Handeln im Kontext des Kulturmanagements ist, in Anlehnung an die Bedingtheit des Wahrgenommenen durch das wahrnehmende Subjekt. ...Der Wellendetektor erkennt Wellen, wo der Teilchendetektor Teilchen erkennt... Das transkulturelle Bewusstsein erkennt Einheit, wo das interkulturelle Diversität erkennt und somit per se integrativ wirkt. Beide sind bewusstseinsrelative komplementäre Aspekte der Wirklichkeit insgesamt, ebenso wie die Welle-Teilchen Dualität.

(30) The metaphorical quantum cultural effect.
1. Die subjektive Integration des inter-transkulturellen Bewusstseinsraumes tendiert dazu, das kulturelle Umfeld zu integrieren.
2. Die subjektive Spaltung des inter-transkulturellen Bewusstseinsraumes tendiert dazu, das kulturelle Umfeld zu spalten.
(die von mir auf der Basis meines transkulturellen 5P - Philosophie-Physik-

Psychologie-Managementansatz - Managementansatzes entwickelte metaphorische quantenkulturelle Formel, die die Qualität des Bewusstseins im hier detaillierten Sinn als Schlüsselvariable allen nachhaltigen Kulturmanagements betrachtet.

(alle naturwissenschaftlichen Axiome werden als Sinnbilder und Metaphern Kulturmanagement-didaktisch eingesetzt)

(31) The perceptual relativity assumption of cultural diversity or the „there is no diversity of culture, there is a diversity of perception" hypothesis.

No cultural diversity but rather a perceptual diversity:

THERE IS NO CULTURAL DIVERSITY

THERE IS, HOWEVER, A DIVERSITY OF THE DEPTH OF PERCEPTION OF EXISTENCE!

The experience of diversity arises as a consequence of a lopsided perception that ignores or refuses to perceive the wholeness of existence referred to metaphorically as the cultural complementarity principle of unity and diversity that has an inkling of the integrality and integrity of creation. The cultural spell under which the world presently is appears therefore as a consequence of perception that is a culture consciousness with limited awareness. Culture seen as such is an act of consciousness. And the type of culture consciousness a player has cocreates the cultural reality within and around him.

From there one may even infer that culture being an act of consciousness based on perception and awareness it cannot be conceived of apart from the human dimension of consciousness. The cultural discourse that fills libraries and the pockets of culture gurus and the lecture halls of universities alike is based on a culture paradigm that cannot have any permanence and sustainable impact on globalization. If it is not enhanced and complemented it can mislead the whole world as fascism and communism have misled the millions and the masses until they were put in their true context and understood more fully. If culture that some assume holds the place of these worldviews and errors of the past at present is not put in its true context likewise it may have the same impact and destiny as those cultural errors. Therefore the present cultural paradigm imperatively requires the correction and completion of its edifice, which is the purpose of the inquiry.

This epistemological perception of culture and cultural diversity does not altogether eclipse the practical value of cultural diversity. The first is helpful in cultural problem solving, the second for evolving. Its dialectics help the world to grow and develop based on the dialectics of diversity. When that causes problems the complementary epistemological perception of culture can be used as a cultural problem solver. So the epistemological and the pragmatic standpoint are the complementary aspects of a culture theory and management practice in accordance with man and his needs. And it does neither sacrifice uniqueness to a heresy of an irenology of misconstrued equality, nor unity to unbridgeable diversity.

(32) The Transcultural Profiler Model: a universal model for culture and intercultural management, derived from a 5D/5P transcultural/transdisciplinary approach and integrated top-bottom based on sound principles.

DER TRANSKULTURELLE PROFILER

Code	Label	Layer
12.1-12.12	Planetary interface	geological interface
11.1-11.12	Trust	basic
10.1-10.12	Competencies	foundation
9.1-9.12	Corporate profile	ground
8.1-8.12	Communication profile	windows
7.1-7.12	National culture profile	walls
6.1-6.12	Individual culture profile	
5.1-5.12	Evolution	cupola
4.1-4.12	Ethics	
3.1-3.12	Operation-alisation	
2.1-2.12	Noetics	
1.1-1.12	Cosmic Interface	lantern

Planetary interface	Trust	Competencies	Corporate profile	Communication profile	National culture profile	Individual culture profile	Evolution
International law	Competence	Altruism	Specialist job	High/Low context	High PDI/Low PDI	Family	Sensory
Biodiversity	Compatibility	Transcultural mindset	Level of literacy	Public/Private space	Individualism/Collectivism	Religion	Activeness
Sustainability	Benevolence	Openness	Training	Free/Contr. information	Strong UA/Weak UA	Education	Affectiveness
Climate change impact	Integrity	Flexibility	Organizational culture	Poly-/Monochronic	Masculinity/Femininity	Language	Analytical
Int. political equilibrium	Predictability	Personal autonomy	Operational field	Direct/Indirect	Long/Short-term orientation	Profession	Synthetic
Int. economic equilib.	Sincerity	Emotional strength	Scale of operations	Affective/Instrumental	Individualism/Communit	Class	Universalism→Ethics→ Operation-→Noetics→ Cosmic Interface
Cultural equilibrium	Open with information		Institutional environm.	Abstract/Concrete	Universalism/Particularism	Gender	Denial
Strategic balance	Accessible	Perception	Leadership orientation	Private/Public	Achievement/Ascription	Race	Definite
Genetic heritage integrity	Reciprocal	Listening orientation	Management style	Linear/Circular	Specific/Diffuse	Generation	Minimalis.
Intercultural ethics	Moral responsibility	Transparency	Motivation	Intellectual/Relational	Emotional/Neutral	Neighbourhood	Acceptance
Environm. compatibility	Inclusion	Cultural knowledge	Corporate model	Succinct/Elaborate	Internal/External	Friends	Adaptation
Resource impact	Good intentions	Influencing	Synergy	Cultural distance	Contextual/Personal	Sequential/Synchronous	Region	Integration

Planetary interface	Trust	Competencies	Corporate profile	Communication profile	National culture profile	Evolution				
Environmental compatibility check	Trust is the foundation of human relationships	Special intercultural competencies	The corporate environment constitutes the business needs on which intercultural relationships must be based	Walls and windows determine the degree to which we build up barriers or make them permeable and open /close windows for communication		Shoulders define and consolidate the design	Refines	Enhances	Activates	Integrates	Transcends

21

Cultural T-Man

or

The τ(TAU)-Model of Culture for Global Culture Management

ETHICS

Awareness - Knowledge - Skills - Practice

UNITY

DIVERSITY

SYNERGY

CREATIVITY

INNOVATION

PROSPERITY

INTEGRITY

Die Konvergenz der horizontalen und der vertikalen Achsen versinnbildlicht die Integration der interkulturellen Ausbildungs-(horizontale Achse) und Managementprozesse (vertikale Achse) im alle Diversität integrierenden Prinzip der Einheit. Vergl. obere Dimensionen des transkulturellen Profilers.

(34) A Synopsis of Modern Intercultural Studies

Generation	Typology	Cultural Optic
• Generation: Hofstede/deterministic		What's the cultural profile?
• G.: Trompenaars, Hampden-Turner	deterministic/indeterministic	How do I handle culture?
• G.: Brannen and Salk indeterministic		How can I optimize it?
• G.: Transculturalism indet./creatively probabilistic		What is the nature of the perception of culture as such?

1980ies	90ies+	3rd millennium
Cross-cultural comparative	intercultural	transcultural
Static	dynamic	integrative meta-level
Taxonomy	action-oriented	integrative
Psychosomatic level	idem	noetic/transcultural level

Finally, I would like to sum up the totality of intercultural research at a paradigmatic level:

Determinism	Indeterminism	Probabilism
Newton	Quantum mechanics	Modern physics
Hofstede THT (transition)	Brannen and Salk	Transcultural
Aggregate models	Negotiated culture	Integrated culture

(It highlights intercultural management paradigm evolution based on natural science paradigm changes)

(35) A Holistic Human Intelligence Model

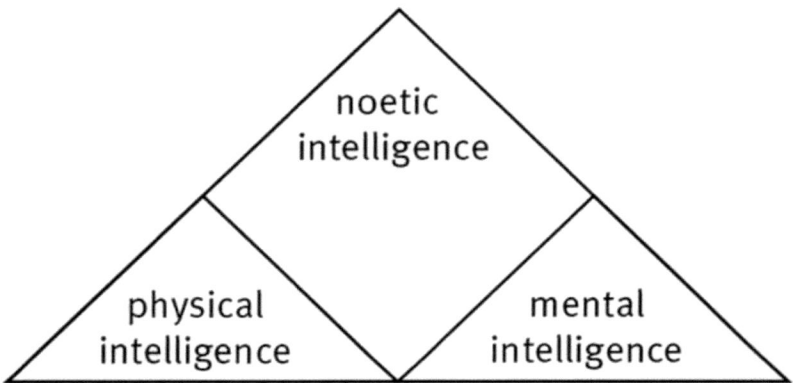

(36) 360° Transcultural Synergy Model

360° Transcultural Synergy Legend

DIMENSIONS	STRATEGIES	SYNERGIES	POTENTIALITIES
D1/2 Culture A/B	1 Avoidance	1 Coordinate 0/0	1 Culture mismanagement, denial
D1/2 Culture A/B	2 Dominance	2 Coordinate 10/0	2 Culture mismanagement, lopsided
D1/2 Culture A/B	3 Accommodation	3 Coordinate 0/10	3 Culture mismanagement, lopsided
D3/4 Time/Cult. Space	4 Compromise	4 Coordinate 5/5	4 Culture standard, corrupted values
D5 Synergy 90°	5 Reconciliation	5 Coordinate 10/10	5 Real potentiality
D6 Ethics 180°	6 Ethical Synergy	6 Coordinate 10+/10+	6 Advanced real potentialities
D7/8 Noetics 240°/360°	7 Noetic Synergy	7 Coordinate ∞	7 Infinite transcultural Potentialities

(D7 means thinking together beyond concepts, images, conclusions, positions, beliefs, personal psychological commitments to resolve a conflict rooted in the mind and consciousness)

360° Transcultural Synergy

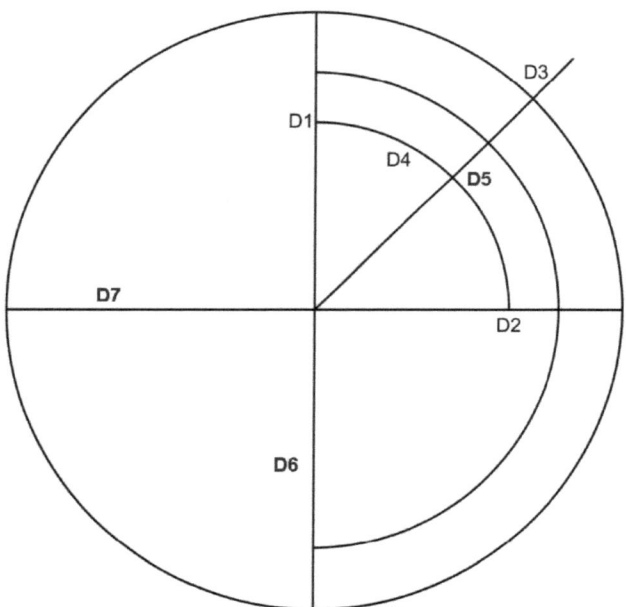

(37) Maßgaben für das Management globaler virtueller Teams

1.Unterschiede im Bereich des Führungsstils: Straffer versus lockerer Führungsstil

2. Unterschiede im Bereich des Entscheidungsprozesses

3. Unterschiede im Bereich der Vertrauensbildung

4. Unterschiede im Bereich der Kommunikation

Basierend auf der globalen virtuellen Team Forschung von Erin Meyer (und Professoren Kollegen), adjunct professor of organizational behavior at INSEAD, France und The Four Keys to Success with Virtual Teams (Forbes - 19th August 2010)

(38) Memory-Anticipation Model

Bild 2. Quelle: Universität Cambridge. Memory-Anticipation Model, 2004. Persönliche Arbeitsunterlagen des Autors.

BIBLIOGRAPHY

Adler, N (2002) *International Dimensions of Organizational Behavior*, South-Western, Cincinnati, Oh. ISBN: 0-324-05786-5

Apfelthaler, G (2002) *Interkulturelles Management: Die Bewältigung interkultureller Differenzen in der internationalen Unternehmenstätigkeit.* Manz, Wien

Audia, PG and Tams, S (2002) 'Goal Setting, Performance Appraisal, Feedback' in Gannon, M J and Newman, L (Eds.) *The Blackwell Handbook of Cross-Cultural Management*, Blackwell Publishers, Oxford. ISBN: 0-631-21430-5

Bartlett, CH and Goshal, S and Birkinshaw (2003) *Transnational Management. Text, Cases, and Readings in Cross-Border Management*, International Edition, McGraw-Hill/Irwine, New York, NY. ISBN: 007-123228-1

Belbin (1996) *Team Roles at Work.* Butterworth-Heinemann

Bond (1988) *The Cross-Cultural Challenge to Social Psychology.* Books on Demand.

Brannen MY and Salk JE (2000) Partnering Across Borders: Negotiating organizational culture in a German-Japanese joint venture, *Human Relations*, Volume 53(4) 451- 487, Sage Publications, London

Brosse, T (1984). *La Conscience-Energie. Structure de l'Homme et de l'Univers. Ses implications scientifiques, sociales et spirituelles.* Editions Présence. Sisteron. ISBN 2-901696-15-5

Davison, S C, Ward K (1999) *Leading International Teams.* McGraw-Hill. Maidenhead. ISBN: 0 07 709209 4.

Delahaye, Y (1977) *La Frontière Et Le Texte*, Payot, Paris. ISBN: 2-228-11850-09

Ewington, N (2004) *Workbook Unit 1, Workbook unit 2 and Workbook Unit 3*, CPI University of Cambridge, UK

Ghemawat, P (2001) Distance Still Matters. The Hard Reality of Global Expansion. *Harvard Business Review.* September 2001

Goodall, K and Roberts, J (2003) Repairing Managerial Knowledge-Ability over Distance. Organisation Studies 24 (7): 1153 – 1175, Sage Publications, London

Goodall, K and Roberts, J (2003) Only connect: teamwork in the multinational. *Journal of World Business* 38 (2003) 150-164, Pergamon

Goodall, K (2002) Managing to Learn: from cross-cultural theory to education practice, Warner M and Joynt P (Eds.) *Managing Across Cultures: Issues and Perspectives.* Thompson Learning

Govindarajan, V and Gupta A K (2001) Building an Effective Global Business Team, *MIT Sloan Management Review*, Summer 2001

Hampden-Turner, Ch and *Trompenaars*, F (2002) *Building Cross-Cultural Competence. How to create wealth from conflicting values*, John Wiley and Sons Ltd, Chichester, England. ISBN: 0-471-49527-1

Hall, E (1990) *Beyond Culture.* Anchor

Hersey, P and Blanchard, K H (1993) *Management of Organizational Behaviour: Utilizing Human Resources, 6th edition*, Prentice Hall

Hickson, DJ and Pugh, DS (2001) *Management Worldwide. Distinctve Styles Amid Globalization*, Penguin Books Ltd, London. ISBN: 0-14100603-X.

Hodgetts, R M and Luthan, F (2003): *International Management: culture, strategy, and behaviour*, Boston, Mass., McGraw-Hill

Hofstede, G (1980) *Culture's Consequences, International Differences in Work-Related Values*, Sage Publications, Newbury Park, Ca. ISBN: 0-8039-1444-

Hofstede, G (2002) *Cultures and Organizations. Intercultural Cooperation and its Importance for Survival. Software of the Mind*, Profile Books Ltd, London. ISBN: 1-86197-543-

Hofstede, G (2003) *Culture and Organizations. Intercultural Cooperation and its Importance for Survival, Software of the Mind, Profile Books Ltd, London*. ISBN: 1 8697 543 0

Hofstede, G and Hofstede, G J (2005) *Culture and Organizations. Intercultural Cooperation and its Importance for Survival, Software of the Mind*, McGraw-Hill: ISBN: 0-07-143959-5

Holden, N (2004) *German as a Language of Management: Pragmatic Observations of German-style Networking and Knowledge-Sharing*, Interknow Workshop II, Regensburg.

Knapp, K (1996) 'Interpersonale und interkulturelle Kommunikation' in Bergemann, N (Ed.) *Interkulturelle Kommunikation*, Physica-Verlag, Heidelberg. ISBN: 3-7908-0913-6

Krishnamurti, Jiddu. Various Talks across the world. Personal attendance.

Maisonrouge J (1988) *Inside IBM. A European's Story*. Collins. London. ISBN: 0-00-217692-0

Mole, J (1993) *Mind your Manners. Managing Culture Clash in the Single European Market*, Industrial Society Press, London. ISBN: 1 85788 000 5

Mullins, L J (2002) *Management and Organisational Behaviour, 6th edition*, Prentice Hall

Naipaul V S. (1984) *Finding the Centre*, Penguin Books Ltd. Harmondsworth, Middlesex, England

Price, S (2000) 'A View from a Bridge: Stereotypes of the German in Business and Higher Education' in Emig, R (Ed.) Stereotypes in Contemporary Anglo-German Relations', Macmillan Press Ltd, Basingstoke. ISBN: 0-333-79341-2

Steers, R and Sanchez-Runde, C (2002) 'Culture, Motivation, and Work Bahavior' in
Gannon, M J and Newman, K L (Eds.) *The Blackwell Handbook of Cross-Cultural
Management, Blackwell Publishers,* Oxford. ISBN: 0-631-21430-5

Singh, D Talks across the World. Personal listening

Singh, R Talks and Conferences. Personal attendance

Stuart, R and Barsoux, JL and Kieser, A and Ganter, HD and Wagenbach, P (1994)
Managing in Britain and in Germany, The Macmillan Press Ltd, Basingstoke.
ISBN: 0-312-12237-3

Triandis, H C (2002) 'Generic Individualism and Collectivism' in Gannon, M J and
Newman, KL (Eds.) *The Blackwell Handbook of Cross-Cultural Management,*
Blackwell Publishers Ltd, Oxford. ISBN: 0-631-21430-5

Tsuda, I Personal Acquaintance and Cahiers de Tsuda

Weidenfeld, G (1999) "Englisches Deutschlandbild" in *Die Politische Meinung,* Volume 358,
Nr.10, pp 55-62. ISSN: 00323446.

Yong, L and Kammhuber, S (2003) 'Ostasien: China' (East-Asia: China) in Thomas, A and
Kinast, U and Schroll-Machl, S (Eds.) *Handbuch der Internationalen Kommunikation und
Kooperation, Band 1. (Handbook of International Communication and Cooperation, Volume
1)* Vandenhoeck & Ruprecht, Goettingen. ISBN: 3-525-46172-0.

Worldwork (2002) *International Management Development. The International Profiler,*
London